Prime Ministers of Canada

Contemporary Canada

By Bev Cline

Weigl

CALGARY
www.weigl.com

Published by Weigl Educational Publishers Limited
6325 10 Street SE
Calgary, Alberta, Canada
T2H 2Z9

Website: www.weigl.com
Copyright © 2007 WEIGL EDUCATIONAL PUBLISHERS LIMITED

Library and Archives Canada Cataloguing in Publication

Rossiter, Mary Juanita
        Contemporary Canada / Mary Juanita Rossiter.
(Prime ministers of Canada)
Includes index.
ISBN 1-55388-256-3 (bound).--ISBN 1-55388-247-4 (pbk.)
        1. Prime ministers--Canada--Biography--Textbooks.
2. Canada--History--1963- --Textbooks. I. Title. II. Series:
Prime ministers of Canada (Calgary, Alta.)
FC26.P7R68 2006   971.064'70922   C2006-902488-X

Printed in Canada
1 2 3 4 5 6 7 8 9 0 10 09 08 07 06

Cover: Brian Mulroney was born March 20, 1939, in Quebec. He was first elected prime minister in 1984.

Photo Credits: Canadian Press: page 16; **Glenbow Museum Archives:** page 5 (nc-6-11899); **Library and Archives Canada:** pages 4 (C-005327, C-010460, PA-033933, C-001971), 5 (C-00687, PA-128175); **Saskatchewan Archives:** page 4 (R-D700); **Courtesy of Vance Rodewalt:** page 20.

We acknowledge the financial support of the Government of Canada through the Book Publishing Industry Development Program (BPIDP) for our publishing activities.

Project Coordinator
Tatiana Tomljanovic

Design
Terry Paulhus

All of the Internet URLs given in the book were valid at the time of publication. However, due to the dynamic nature of the Internet, some addresses may have changed, or sites may have ceased to exist since publication. While the author and publisher regret any inconvenience this may cause readers, no responsibility for any such changes can be accepted by either the author or the publisher.

Contents

Canada's Prime Ministers

Since **Confederation**, there have been 22 Canadian prime ministers. Canada's prime ministers have come from many provinces and cultures. Some of them, such as the first prime minister, John A. Macdonald, were born in other countries. They came to Canada because they, or their parents, decided Canada was the best place to live and raise a family.

Canada's prime ministers are people of many talents and different interests. Some trained as lawyers, while others were journalists, doctors, farmers, writers, teachers, business people, and members of the **civil service**. Some of them fought as soldiers to protect Canada and her allies. All of them had one thing in common. They wanted to make Canada one of the best places in the world to live.

THE NEW NATION (CONFEDERATION TO 1896)

 John A. Macdonald
(July 1, 1867–November 5, 1873; October 17, 1878–June 6, 1891)

 Alexander Mackenzie
(November 7, 1873–October 8, 1878)

 John J. C. Abbott
(June 16, 1891–November 24, 1892)

 John S. D. Thompson
(December 5, 1892–December 12, 1894)

 Mackenzie Bowell
(December 21, 1894–April 27, 1896)

 Charles H. Tupper
(May 1, 1896–July 8, 1896)

TURN OF THE 20ᵀᴴ CENTURY (1896–1920)

 Wilfrid Laurier
(July 11, 1896–October 6, 1911)

 Robert L. Borden
(October 10, 1911–July 10, 1920)

TIME OF TURMOIL (1920–1948)

Arthur Meighen
(July 10, 1920–December 29, 1921; June 29, 1926–September 25, 1926)

Richard B. Bennett
(August 7, 1930–October 23, 1935)

William Lyon Mackenzie King
(December 29, 1921–June 28, 1926; September 25, 1926–August 7, 1930; October 23, 1935–November 15, 1948)

TIME OF TRANSITION (1948–1968)

TRUDEAU ERA (1968–1984)

Louis S. Saint Laurent
(November 15, 1948–June 21, 1957)

Pierre Elliott Trudeau
(April 20, 1968–June 3, 1979; March 3, 1980–June 30, 1984)

John George Diefenbaker
(June 21, 1957–April 22, 1963)

Charles Joseph Clark
(June 4, 1979–March 2, 1980)

Lester B. Pearson
(April 22, 1963–April 20, 1968)

John N. Turner
(June 30, 1984–September 17, 1984)

CONTEMPORARY CANADA (1984 TO PRESENT)

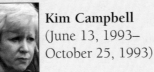

Martin Brian Mulroney
(September 17, 1984–June 13, 1993)

Jean J. Chrétien
(October 25, 1993–December 12, 2003)

Kim Campbell
(June 13, 1993–October 25, 1993)

Paul E. P. Martin
(December 12, 2003–February 6, 2006)

Stephen J. Harper
(February 6, 2006–)

Modern-Day Canada

Mulroney, one of Canada's most controversial prime ministers, led the country for nine years.

In a period of about 20 years, Canada had five prime ministers—Brian Mulroney, Kim Campbell, Jean Chrétien, Paul Martin, and Stephen Harper. These people governed in a society increasingly dominated by advances in technology. In this changing world, borders were re-examined, and the world did not seem as big a place as it was 50 years ago. The face of Canada was redefined during this period.

Aboriginal and French issues were predominant. The Oka crisis, an conflict over Aboriginal land, made Canadians more aware of Aboriginal issues and helped pave the way for the creation of a new northern **territory**, Nunavut. This new territory set a precedent in Aboriginal land claims and resulted in a new focus on Canada's North.

Francophone issues also dominated this period. A **referendum** for the province of Quebec to separate from Canada was held in Quebec, but ultimately was rejected. Although Mulroney and Chrétien both came from working class families in Quebec, neither were able to find a solution for the separation issues in their home province.

Many prime ministers entered and left office during the end of the 20th and beginning of the 21st centuries, each affecting a country that has become more modern and secure in its **multicultural** identity.

In 1993, Mulroney officially resigned from politics and returned to his law practice.

Keeping Canada Together

"I am honoured to inform the House that at about 10 p.m. last night the Premiers and I reached unanimous agreement in principle on a Constitutional package which will allow Quebec to rejoin the Canadian constitutional family."
*Mulroney addressing the **House of Commons** on the Meech Lake **Accord**, May 1, 1987*

Brian Mulroney: The Businessman

> "I think that history will record that, further on down the road, Mr. Mulroney's greatest achievement was the fact that he dragged Canada, kicking and screaming, into the 21st Century."
>
> *Don Mazankovski, former* **cabinet minister**

Prime Minister-Elect
Brian Mulroney

Brian Mulroney was a successful lawyer and businessman before he entered politics. Unlike most other prime ministers, he was never a career politician. He was, however, a colourful speaker, and a passionate, funny, and sincere Canadian.

During his time in office, Mulroney was one of Canada's most popular prime ministers. In 1997, *Maclean's Magazine* reported that 25 scholars had ranked Brian Mulroney eighth out of 20 prime ministers. However, when he resigned as prime minister, Mulroney's popularity dwindled to 20 percent in the polls. He had failed to get the provinces to approve a new constitution.

Mulroney's popularity suffered partially because he was unable to make Quebec happy with its status in Canada's Constitution. He devoted much of time to his home province of Quebec, but in the end, was unsuccessful in satisfying **Quebeckers'** requests. Mulroney also introduced new taxes that many Canadians did not like.

Still, Mulroney worked to improve Canada's multicultural identity and to protect the environment. In 1990, Mulroney appointed Ramon "Ray" John Hnatyshyn as **governor general** of Canada. Hnatyshyn was the first Ukrainian-born governor general. He is remembered for re-opening the grounds of Rideau Hall, the official residence of the governor general, to the public and inviting Canadians in for concerts, picnics, and skating.

The 1984 election of Brian Mulroney as prime minister of Canada ended close to 16 years of Liberal Party rule that was interrupted for only 6 months in 1979.

Mulroney also established a close relationship with the United States. He felt that Canadian economic success could only be secured by access to foreign markets. Mulroney achieved that success through the 1988 Free Trade Agreement.

In 1992, Canada, along with the United States and Mexico, launched the North American Free Trade Agreement (NAFTA) and formed the world's largest free trade area. NAFTA has brought economic growth and rising standards of living for people in all three countries.

"In 20 minutes we finished the interview and turned off the camera. Once again, Mulroney's animation returned. He told us stories about his first time in the House of Commons, his many confrontations with Trudeau, his accomplishments as prime minister, his commitment to Quebec. For a full hour we were audience to a fascinating display by a passionate, funny, sometimes angry, often defensive, but sincere Canadian."

Noni Maté, journalist

In 1992, Canadian Prime Minister Brian Mulroney, U.S. President George Bush, and Mexican President Salinas de Gortari gathered together in San Antonio, Texas, to launch NAFTA.

The Boy From Baie-Comeau

"Before the GST [Goods and Services Tax] and before Free Trade, Brian Mulroney was a small-town boy who announced at age 29 that he would one day be Prime Minister."
Rae Murphy, Robert Chodos, and Nick Auf der Maur, authors of The Boy from Baie-Comeau

Martin "Brian" Mulroney was born on March 20, 1939, in Baie-Comeau, Quebec. He was the third child of Benedict and Irene Mulroney's six children. His father was an electrician at the local paper mill.

At the age of 14, Mulroney left Baie-Comeau to attend high school at St. Thomas Roman Catholic boarding school in Chatham, New Brunswick. After high school, he entered St. Francis Xavier University in Antigonish, Nova Scotia, where he studied political science.

While at school, Mulroney served as prime minister of St. Francis Xavier's student government. He was also vice-chairperson of the Youth for Diefenbaker committee and attended the 1956 Progressive Conservative (PC) leadership convention. The leader at the time, John Diefenbaker, captivated Mulroney.

Mulroney graduated with a bachelor of arts degree with honours in 1959. Shortly after, he began working towards his law degree at Dalhousie University in Halifax. After one year of study, he transferred to the University of Laval in Quebec City, where he studied **civil law**.

The origins of Mulroney's university, the University of Laval, can be traced back to Monseigneur François de Laval who founded the Séminaire de Quebec with the authorization of King Louis XIV of France in 1663.

While at Laval, Mulroney continued his involvement with the **Conservative Party**'s youth wing. He was elected vice-president of the Conservative Students' Federation. By 1961, he was a student advisor to Diefenbaker on Quebec affairs. He also became acquainted with the president of the Student Federation, the future Prime Minister Joe Clark.

After graduation from Laval, Mulroney began working at a Montreal law firm. By the mid-1970s, he gained celebrity status in Quebec for investigating crime in the construction industry while working for the Cliché **Commission**.

Mulroney married Mila Pivnink on May 26, 1973. Mila had been born in Sarajevo, Yugoslavia. She moved with her parents to Montreal when she was five years old. As a stay-at-home mother, Mila appealed to many female voters. She was seen as the perfect political wife. Mila impressed people with her quick wit and organizational skills. Brian and Mila had four children—Nicholas, Mark, Benedict, and Caroline.

DID YOU KNOW?

Benedict "Ben" Mulroney, has a history degree from Duke University and a law degree from the University of Laval. Many Canadians recognize Ben as the host of CTV's *Canadian Idol* and co-host of *etalk Daily*.

Brian Mulroney met his wife, Mila, just before her 19th birthday. They were married by the time Mila was 20.

Mulroney: Becoming Prime Minister

"He had this wonderful, large-hearted, Irish capacity to be afraid neither of celebration nor of sadness, and to really embrace both. I think part of why people in the Party were so loyal to him over the years was really because they felt that he had been quite loyal to them. He made them feel quite important as individuals."

Hugh Segal, policy advisor and former chief of staff to Mulroney

In 1974, Progressive Conservative Party leader Robert Stanfield lost the federal election to Pierre Trudeau and stepped down as leader. Brian Mulroney ran for the leadership of the Conservative Party, but he lost to Joe Clark. Although Mulroney was well-known in Quebec, he was not yet known in the rest of Canada.

After years of campaigning and increasing his visibility in Canada, Mulroney became leader of the PC party in 1983. Fifteen months later, on September 17, 1984, Mulroney was elected as prime minister of Canada. His party won 211 out of 251 seats. It was a landslide victory. The Progressive

In 1984, in Mulroney's home province of Quebec, the Conservatives won 58 of the 75 ridings.

Conservative Party had won the largest majority of seats in Canadian history. It was the first Conservative Party majority government in 22 years. The election victory was attributed to new support in Quebec for the Conservative Party and its Quebec-born **bilingual** leader.

When Mulroney came to office as prime minister, Canada's economy was strong, and unemployment was low. However, the previous administration had spent more money than it

had collected in taxes. During Mulroney's second term in office, Canada's economy declined. Taxes were increased. In 1991, the government introduced a new tax called the Goods and Services Tax, which became known as the GST. The government hoped the tax would stimulate the economy.

Despite the GST, the economy continued to flounder. The decline of cod stocks in Atlantic Canada resulted in the Mulroney government having to impose a **moratorium** on the cod fishery. This collapsed a large portion of Newfoundland's fishing industry and caused serious economic hardship in the province.

Nearly 11 years after Mulroney's moratorium on the cod fishery, the federal government announced on April 23, 2003, an outright closure of whatever cod fishing remained. Mature cod stockpiles had dipped nearly 97 percent below the 1990 levels.

DEFINING MOMENT

Canada's anti-**apartheid** stand was toughened after Mulroney's election in 1984. Canada restricted its trade with South Africa. Mulroney's opposition to apartheid put him at odds with the leaders of Great Britain and the United States but won him respect elsewhere. Stephen Lewis, the United Nations Special Envoy for HIV/AIDS in Africa, said that Mulroney showed leadership in the fight against apartheid.

Constitutional Issues

"In the province of Quebec he was able to speak to the people as one of the people. Mulroney has, obviously, a gift for language and he speaks Quebec French—he doesn't speak Parisian French, he doesn't speak upper class French—he speaks ordinary French. I don't mean to say it's incorrect, necessarily, but he speaks the language of the people and the language of the street."

Robert Bothwell, historian

DEFINING MOMENT

Mulroney had known Lucien Bouchard since they studied at Laval University. Mulroney appointed Bouchard ambassador to France in 1988. He also appointed him secretary of state and, later, minister of the environment. Bouchard became frustrated with Brian Mulroney and the Conservative Party after the Meech Lake Accord. He resigned from the Conservative Party on May 21, 1990.

Within weeks, he had gathered other members of **Parliament** from Quebec to form the Bloc Québécois. The Bloc represents the interests of Québécois, French-speaking Quebeckers, in federal Parliament. In the 1993 federal election, the Bloc won 54 seats and became the official opposition in Ottawa.

After being elected in 1984, Mulroney sought to erase the conflict between Quebec and the rest of Canada. He believed that recognition of Quebec's special status in a new constitution would bring the province into agreement with the rest of Canada.

THE MEECH LAKE ACCORD

The Meech Lake Accord was Mulroney's attempt to recognize Quebec's special status within the Constitution. In April 1987, Mulroney and Canada's 10 provincial leaders met to discuss changes to the Constitution. The meeting took place at the government's private retreat in Meech Lake, Quebec. The accord granted the provinces more power from the **federal government**. Quebec was also to be recognized as a "distinct society."

Aboriginal Canadians opposed the Meech Lake Accord. They thought that Aboriginal communities should also be seen as distinct societies. Elijah Harper, former chief of the Red Sucker Lake First Nation, was appointed minister responsible for Native affairs in 1986. A year later, he became minister of northern affairs for Manitoba on behalf of Aboriginal interests. Harper prevented the Meech Lake vote from taking place in the Manitoba legislature, effectively ending the accord on behalf of Aboriginal interests.

All the provinces except Newfoundland and Manitoba approved. Without the support of these two provinces, however, the Meech Lake Accord failed. Quebec considered this failure as a rejection by the rest of Canada.

Lucien Bouchard, Mulroney's minister of the environment, had strongly supported the accord. After its rejection, he left the Conservative Party.

THE CHARLOTTETOWN ACCORD

In 1992, Mulroney made a second attempt to get Quebec to accept Canada's constitution. This time, he decided to ask Canadians for their opinions. Committees were created across the country to gather the views of Canadians. Tensions grew. The government of Quebec, led by **Premier** Robert Bourassa, threatened to hold a vote on separatism if the country did not meet Quebec's demands.

After months of discussion, an agreement was reached. The agreement took place in Charlottetown, Prince Edward Island, where the Confederation discussions of 1864 had taken place. On October 26, 1992, the Charlottetown Accord was presented to the Canadian voters. The national referendum resulted in a defeat of the Accord. Fifty-five percent voted "no."

Canada was again caught in a unity crisis. Regionalism in western Canada began to grow, as did Quebec separatism.

Through the Meech Lake and Charlottetown Accords, Mulroney attempted to resolve Quebec's concerns over the Constitution and prevent separation.

DID YOU KNOW?

Mulroney passed Canada's Multiculturalism Act. This act made Canada the first country in the world to pass a law that declared multiculturalism as a fundamental value of society.

Aboriginal Viewpoint

"Look at Nunavut, there wouldn't be a Nunavut, without Oka. We had to suffer for other people's gains. Oka inspired aboriginal people all over Canada."

Kenneth Deer, journalist

THE OKA CRISIS

In 1990, worldwide attention was focussed on what became known as the "Oka crisis." Initiated on March 11, the Oka crisis was the result of a land dispute between the Mohawk Nation **reserve** of Kanesatake and the town of Oka, Quebec. Oka is a village located on the bank of the Ottawa River, near Laval, Quebec.

A Mohawk burial ground and a sacred grove of pine trees is located near Kanesatake. The mayor of Oka announced plans to expand a golf course and build 60 condominiums on this land. These plans were not made in consultation with the Mohawk Nation. In protest, members of the Mohawk community erected a barrier that blocked access to the land. The government sent a Special Weapons Assault Team (SWAT) that attacked the barricade. It is unknown who shot first, but a 30-second gun assault took place. Police Corporal Marcel Lemay was shot and killed.

The 1990 Oka Crisis led to intense face-to-face standoffs between members of the Mohawk Nation and Canadian soldiers.

In an attempt to resolve the situation, Mulroney's government agreed to spend more than $5 million to purchase the land the Mohawks were trying to protect. The Mohawks felt that the government had not addressed the true problem, which was the ownership of the land. The Royal Canadian Mounted Police (RCMP) were brought in to help the Quebec provincial police, but they were unable to establish order. Quebec Premier Robert Bourassa requested help from the Canadian Armed Forces. More than 2,000 troops were sent to Oka. The Mohawks at Oka unexpectedly surrendered on September 26. Thirty-four people from the Oka reserve were arrested by the army.

The Oka crisis had lasted 78 days. The expansion of the golf course was cancelled. International reaction to Canada's handling of the Oka crisis was critical. In 1997, the federal government purchased the disputed land from Oka. The Mohawks were then allowed to expand their existing cemetery. The Oka crisis cost the Quebec government an estimated $180 million, not including the cost of the armed forces.

NUNAVUT

Discussions about dividing the Northwest Territories became a reality in May 1993. As part of an Inuit land claim, Mulroney signed an agreement with the Northwest Territories that promised to divide the land into two regions to create a new territory. It became the largest Aboriginal land claim agreement in Canadian history.

On April 1, 1999, the map of Canada changed. The Northwest Territories was divided in two. *Nunavut*, meaning "our land" in the Inuktitut language, was created.

Nunavut stretches more than one million square kilometres and covers an area twice as large as British Columbia. Approximately 27,000 live there, and 85 percent of the population are Inuit. Iqaluit is the capital city.

The Oka crisis and Nunavut Settlement Agreement of the early 1990s were both significant events for Aboriginal Canadians. The creation of the Nunavut Territory was a breakthrough with respect to land claims.

The flag of Nunavut is yellow, red, and white, with a blue star. It symbolizes the riches of the land, sea, and sky.

Environmental Issues

"When you get to my age, after you've been Prime Minister for a long time, you look back on certain things and you say… Why did I do this when I should've done that. I don't feel that way about the environment. I think there are a lot of things we missed, but I think we did a lot of the big things that we should have. And I'm glad we did."
Mulroney, 2005

Mulroney strengthened Canada's relationship with the United States. He had a good relationship with both President Ronald Reagan and his successor President George Bush. Mulroney felt that **conservation** was an important part of Canada's political heritage. He therefore saw the importance of Canada working with the United States to protect the environment.

In the early 1980s, **acid rain** became a concern in eastern Canada. Mulroney initiated a plan called the Eastern Canada Acid Rain Program. Its objective was to reduce the sulphur dioxide emissions that caused 2.3 million tonnes of acid rain per year. The program focussed on the seven most eastern provinces. However, much of Eastern Canada's acid rain was formed by U.S. industries and vehicles. Mulroney raised Canadian concern about acid rain during a speech to the United States Congress in April 1984. The speech helped convince the United States to reduce sulphur emissions. In 1988, the Canada-U.S. Acid Rain **Treaty** was established. It is viewed today as a milestone in environmental protection.

Mulroney also established Canada's Green Plan for a Healthy Environment in 1990. It contained policies, programs, and standards to clean up Canada's air, water, parks, and Arctic.

Political cartoons drawn in the 1980s poked fun at the tension between Canadians and Americans on acid rain. Some Canadian cartoons made fun of U.S.-created pollution.

In 1991, Mulroney and Bush signed the Canada-U.S. Air Quality Agreement. Each country agreed to provide air quality reports to the other to prove that they were living up to the clean air agreement. Between 1980 and 1996, U.S. sulphur emissions dropped 27 percent. It is projected that by 2010, the emissions will drop 40 percent.

In 2005, *Corporate Knights*, a Canadian magazine on responsible business, voted Mulroney the "Greenest Prime Minister" in history because of his success in working with the United States on reducing acid rain and improving air quality.

DEFINING MOMENT

In the 1980s, water and soil systems in eastern Canada were affected by acid rain. Many lakes lost their plant and fish life. It has been estimated that acid rain has caused more than $1 billion damage every year. Large forests in eastern Canada have been damaged. Quebec's maple syrup production has been reduced and the salmon habitat severely depleted.

Reflecting on how he was able to get the President George Bush and the Americans to pass the Acid Rain Treaty, Mulroney said, "it required persistence and understanding of the American system, what moves people, understanding interest groups, the media, the House, the Senate, and the Presidential function in all of this."

Mulroney's Legacy

> "Mulroney was probably the first prime minister of Canada who did not see the United States as a threat to Canada."
>
> *Mary Lou Finlay, journalist*

Brian Mulroney was prime minister for nine years. He established positive economic and environmental relations with the United States through agreements such as NAFTA and the Acid Rain Treaty. He also worked towards satisfying Quebec concerns in amending the Constitution with the failed Charlottetown and Meech Lake Accords. Although Mulroney failed in ratifying a new constitution that pleased all provinces and territories, he played a pivotal role in federal recognition of Aboriginal Peoples' land claims when he created the territory of Nunavut.

Prime Minister Mulroney was a prominent figure on the international stage as well. His stand against apartheid in South Africa, and his environmental activism earned worldwide respect.

Mulroney and U.S. President George Bush had a friendly relationship that remained strong through their terms as the leaders of Canada and the United States.

Mulroney enhanced his international recognition as a **statesman** after leaving office. Following his time as prime minister, he continued his career as a successful lawyer, and became a global entrepreneur and a political speaker. He was invested as a Companion of the Order of Canada in 1998.

DEFINING MOMENT

Mulroney was co-chairman of the United Nation's first World **Summit** on Children and an architect of the first Francophone Summit "Sommet de **la Francophonie**" in Paris.

Children and adults gathered at a rally in Central Park, New York City, in 1990 for the United Nation's World Summit on Children. World leaders, including Mulroney, signed the World Declaration on Survival, Protection and Development of Children.

Kim Campbell: Canada's First Woman Prime Minister

Kim Campbell was the first female prime minister in Canada. Before becoming prime minister, she studied political science and lectured at various universities.

Canadians know Avril Phaedra Douglas Campbell as "Kim" Campbell. She was not fond of any of her given names and adopted the name "Kim" when she was teenager in British Columbia.

Campbell studied political science and law at the University of British Columbia. She studied Soviet government at the London School of Economics. She became a lawyer in 1984 and practised law in Vancouver until 1986.

Campbell came to office with much more political experience than Pierre Trudeau, Joe Clark, or Brian Mulroney. In 1981, she was elected to the Vancouver School Board. Two years later, she ran unsuccessfully for British Columbia's Social Credit Party. In 1985, she became policy advisor to British Columbia's premier, Bill Bennett.

In 1988, Campbell was elected to Parliament. As Canada's first woman justice minister, she made significant changes to the **criminal code**. In 1991, she sponsored stricter gun controls in Canada. Campbell also strengthened women's legal protection.

Campbell was elected Conservative Party leader in June 1993. Similar to John Turner, her time as prime minister was dominated by an election campaign. She tried to separate herself from the legacy left by Brian Mulroney, but many Canadians felt the two were too much alike. She was frequently greeted by the chant, "Kim, Kim, you're just like him."

In November 1993, the Conservative Party suffered the worst defeat in Canadian history. The party went from having 154 seats to only two. Without the minimum requirement of 10 seats, the Conservative Party no longer had official party status. Campbell was defeated in her own **riding**. She resigned as party leader.

Although Campbell was only in office for slightly more than four months, she holds the distinction of being Canada's first woman prime minister. She continues to remain active in politics and champions women's rights. She taught political science at Harvard University, served as consul general to Los Angeles, and chaired the Council of Women World Leaders, and has acted as president of the International Women's Forum.

Campbell is an avid supporter of women's rights and has acted as president of the International Women's Forum.

Keeping Canada Together

"In a democracy, government isn't something that a small group of people do to everybody else, it's not even something they do for everybody else, it should be something they do with everybody else."
Campbell, March 25, 1993

Jean Chrétien:
The Little Guy from Shawinigan

Jean Chrétien served as prime minister from 1993 to 2003. Prior to becoming prime minister, he created 10 national parks and appointed the first female justice of the Supreme Court of Canada.

Jean Chrétien came from humble beginnings. He was brought up in a large, working-class family in suburban Quebec. In reference to his humble origins, Chrétien refers to himself as *le petit gars de Shawinigan*—"the little guy from Shawinigan."

When Chrétien became prime minister, he was often criticized for his unpolished style and manner of speaking. For this, he made no apologies. He felt it brought him closer to the working-class people. He did not use a limousine. He drove a Chevrolet. He was well-liked, and people trusted him. His popularity lasted a long time.

On September 10, 1957, Jean married Aline Chaîné. They had met on a bus when she was a 16-year-old secretarial school graduate. They were married five years later. Chrétien consulted Aline for both personal and political advice during his years in politics. He often stated that he would know when to call an election only after he consulted Aline.

When Chrétien became prime minister, Canada's economy was stable. He delivered on his campaign promise to "fix" the government's finances. Chrétien won three consecutive majority elections in the House of Commons. He was the first prime minister to do so since Mackenzie King.

However, Chrétien's time in office was not always easy. The 1995 Quebec referendum on separation was Chrétien's most difficult challenge as prime minister. Although Quebec voted to remain in Canada, it was by a narrow margin. Chrétien began to lose the support of his party. Liberal loyalty shifted away from him and toward his finance minister, Paul Martin.

"The art of politics is learning to walk with your back to the wall, your elbows high, and a smile on your face. It's a survival game played under the glare of lights. If you don't learn that you're quickly finished... The press wants to get you. The opposition wants to get you. Even some of the bureaucrats want to get you. They all may have an interest in making you look bad and they all have ambitions of their own."

Chrétien, 1985

Keeping Canada Together

"To understand Jean Chrétien, you have to understand the handicap with which he came into life—you know he was born deaf in one ear; he was partially dyslexic. Then, at the age of 11 or 12, he gets Bells Palsy on the side of his mouth. He's skinny in a town where the big, brawny guys rule the streets, poor families and so on. So, he had all these fantastic number[s] of disadvantages, and this created in Jean Chrétien a determination to prove himself—that he was absolutely extraordinary."

Lawrence Martin, author and journalist

Chrétien: Becoming Prime Minister

"God gave me a physical defect. I've accepted that since I was a kid. When I was a kid people were laughing at me. But I accepted that because God gave me other qualities and I'm grateful."

Chrétien

Joseph Jacques Jean Chrétien was born on January 11, 1934, in Shawinigan Falls, Quebec. His parents, Wellie and Marie Chrétien, had 19 children. Wellie was the principal organizer of the **Liberal Party** in the Shawinigan region. As a young boy, Jean attended political rallies and meetings with his father. By the time he was 15, he had begun campaigning for local Liberal candidates.

The Chrétien family placed a priority on education. Jean attended boarding school from the age of 5 until he was 21. He attended the St. Joseph Seminary at Trois-Rivières and graduated with a Bachelor of Arts in 1955. He went on to study law at the University of Laval. After he graduated, Jean returned to Shawinigan and opened up a law practice.

In 1963, Jean Chrétien was elected to the House of Commons. He was only 29 years old. When he arrived in Ottawa, he could not speak English very well. The majority of his first two years in Parliament were spent learning English.

During his 17 years in office, he was minister of many important departments, including minister of Indian affairs and northern development, industry, trade and commerce, finance, justice and attorney general, social development, and energy and mine resources. Chrétien was the first French Canadian finance minister. When Pierre Trudeau was prime minister, Chrétien was often referred to as his right-hand man.

Chrétien succeeded John Turner as leader of the Liberal Party on June 23, 1990. Three years later, Chrétien became prime minister. The Liberal Party won 176 Seats. With the 1993 election, Chrétien inherited a country that was

DEFINING MOMENT

Jean Chrétien has Bell Palsy, a condition that is caused by a virus that attacks facial nerves. It is not common and occurs in about 11 out of every 10,000 people. It results in the weakness or paralysis of the facial muscle and a distorted facial expression. The condition is named for Sir Charles Bell, a Scottish surgeon who studied the nerves of facial muscles 200 years ago.

deeply in debt. He appointed Paul Martin finance minister and instructed him to reduce the country's spending.

Martin froze government wages, cut the defence and foreign aid budgets, and reduced the number of government employees. In 1997, the Canadian government's debt was significantly reduced.

While the federal government began reducing its debt in 1997, many provincial governments blamed Prime Minister Chrétien and his minister of finance, Paul Martin, for their debts increasing due to cuts in federal funding of provincial programs, such as health care and social security.

"If we look at our history and prime ministers who had a common touch, I think Chrétien in his own way had a bit of that— the little guy from Shawinigan, that was part of his common touch."
Rudyard Griffiths, founder and executive director of the Dominion Institute

Chrétien and Canada's North

"The North is now a central part of our foreign policy. A sense of northernness extends even to Canadians who have never been to the North. More and more often, they appreciate its vulnerability, they understand and appreciate its Aboriginal heritage, its unique rhythms and its environmental fragility. They also understand its growing importance to our security and **prosperity**."

Lloyd Axworthy, Foreign Affairs Minister in the Chrétien government, 2003

Canada's Arctic encompasses approximately 40 percent of the nation's total land mass and is home to about 85,000 residents. The wildlife and Aboriginal Peoples that live there play an important role in the geographic and cultural diversity of Canada.

Chrétien had a strong connection with Canada's North that continued throughout his political career. Before he was prime minister, he was minister of Indian affairs and northern development. He also played a key role in setting up the international Arctic Council in 1996.

The council is made up of eight nations that have land located within the Arctic. These countries include Canada, Denmark, Finland, Iceland, Norway, Russia, Sweden, and the United States. The main purpose of the council is to address social and economic issues with respect to the Arctic, such as pollution, global climate, and the Arctic's natural resources.

Many scientists believe the melting of polar ice and disappearance of icebergs in Canada's North represents a major threat to global climate and northern habitats.

In September 1998, the first ministerial meeting of the Arctic Council was held in Iqaluit, Nunavut. Chrétien's government announced that it was going to examine how its northern territories could be developed.

Chrétien also worked to enhance the security and prosperity of northern Canadians, especially Aboriginal Peoples, with the Northern Dimension of Canada's Foreign Policy (NDFP).On June 8, 2000, Chrétien signed the NDFP, guaranteeing the rights of people living in Canada's North.

DEFINING MOMENT

Inuit carving is an ancient craft that has been practised for thousands of years. In 1949, the Canadian Handicraft Guild introduced Inuit carvings to the world. The Inuit art market began to flourish. No two pieces of Inuit sculpture are ever alike. There are many different techniques and styles. When Chrétien was minister of indian affairs and northern development, he began to collect Inuit carvings. He often gave the carvings as gifts to visiting dignitaries.

When Pope John Paul II visited Canada in 2002, Chrétien gave him an Inuit sculpture of a bear.

The Quebec Referendum

"What is at stake is our country. What is at stake is our heritage. To break up Canada or build Canada. To remain Canadian or no longer be Canadian. To stay or to leave. This is the issue of the referendum"

Chrétien's Address to the Nation, October 25, 1995

A referendum on Quebec sovereignty was held on May 20, 1980. Quebec's provincial government, the **Parti Québécois**, had organized the vote. The Parti Québécois was strongly in favour of separating from the rest of Canada. Under Pierre Trudeau, Chrétien organized the government's "no" campaign. The referendum was defeated by a vote of 60 percent to 40 percent.

After the referendum, Quebec separation seemed to have become a dead issue until Chrétien's time in office, when an almost identical referendum on Quebec sovereignty was held. In

Jacques Parizeau was replaced as premier of Quebec in 1996 by Lucien Bouchard, leader of the Bloc Québécois Party.

In the 1990s, Hank Gigandet designed the duality flag, a Canadian flag with the addition of two blue strips, to represent the francophone population in Canada.

1994, the Parti Québécois won the Quebec provincial election and Jacques Parizeau, leader of the Parti Québécois, became premier. Two days after his election, Parizeau promised Quebeckers a referendum on **sovereignty**. Quebec separation was again a very real issue for Canada.

The days leading up to the vote were tense for all Canadians. Polls indicated that the majority of Quebeckers intended to vote "yes" to separate from Canada. A "unity rally" was organized by the Liberal Party in downtown Montreal on October 27, 1995. All Canadians were invited to attend to show support for a "no" vote. Discounts were offered on train and plane tickets to encourage Canadians to attend. About 100,000 people attended the rally. People came from the Maritimes and as far away as British Columbia. The crowd included several provincial premiers, such as Mike Harris from Ontario, Frank McKenna from New Brunswick, John Savage from Nova Scotia, and Catherine Callbeck from Prince Edward Island. The rally cost and estimated $4.3 million. Organizers called it "the crusade for Canada."

The referendum vote took place on October 30, 1995. The **federalists** won—50.58 percent of the population of Quebec voted "no" and 49.42 percent voted "yes". More than 94 percent of Quebeckers voted in the referendum.

Chrétien's government was criticized for doing very little with respect to the 1995 referendum. The press stated that the government only became involved at the last minute, when polls suggested that the "yes" side could win.

The Quebec separatist movement lost its momentum in 2000, when Chrétien's federal government passed the Clarity Act. The act stated that a province can separate from Canada only after the province's population has had the opportunity to vote on a clear referendum question. The House of Commons would decide if the referendum question was clearly stated or not. The act was created in response to the 1995 Quebec referendum and the ongoing sovereignty movement in that province.

DEFINING MOMENT

The Canadian Unity Flag was first seen at the Montreal unity rally. The unofficial flag represented the unity of francophones with **anglophones**. Blue stripes were added to the red sections of the original Canadian flag to represent the number of French-speaking Canadians. The flags are still seen today throughout Quebec.

Chrétien On the World Stage

The Museum of Anthropology at the campus of the University of British Columbia was selected as the site of the 1997 APEC Conference in Vancouver.

CHRÉTIEN AND TEAM CANADA

The Chrétien government worked to improve Canada's international economic ties. Shortly after coming to power, Chrétien established Team Canada Missions. Chrétien and provincial leaders travelled to many parts of the world in an effort to increase trade and investment, and to create jobs and growth in Canada. The first mission was to China in 1994.

Since 1994, more than 10 Team Canada Missions have been undertaken. Team Canada has visited countries in Asia and South America, as well as Mexico, Russia, Germany, and Japan. These missions attempt to develop long-term trade and investment opportunities for Canadian business in foreign markets.

APEC CONFERENCE

After becoming prime minister, Chrétien extended economic ties to the **Pacific Rim** countries. In 1997, politicians from around the world came to Vancouver to attend an Asia-Pacific Economic Corporation (APEC) conference. Students from the University of British Columbia protested. They wanted human rights to be on the APEC agenda. Many were upset that President Suharto of Indonesia was attending the conference because of his poor human rights record.

The crowd became rowdy. Unable to control the protest, the RCMP pepper sprayed the protesters. Pepper spray temporarily blinds a person, causes uncontrollable coughing and choking, and a painful burning sensation. Many students were arrested and held without charges.

After the incident, the RCMP Complaints Commission held an inquiry.

In August 2001, the RCMP released a report. It indicated that the RCMP had not implemented an effective plan to handle the crowds. The inquiry also stated improper involvement by the federal government had played a role in the incident. The Chrétien government was criticized for having placed economic dealings ahead of Canadians' right to protest.

> "For me, pepper, I put it on my plate."
> *Chrétien's response to the APEC protest in Vancouver, 1997*

The Revolutionary Knitting Circle was created by Grant Neufeld and held in downtown Calgary as a peaceful protest to the 2002 G8 summit in Kananaskis, Alberta.

GROUP OF EIGHT (G8) SUMMIT

The G8 is the most influential group of developed countries in the world including, Britain, France, Germany, Italy, Japan, Russia, the United States, and Canada. The leaders of each of these countries meet once a year. In June 2002, Chrétien hosted the G8 summit in Canada. Previous G8 summits in other countries had come under media attention due to protests. One person had been killed and 50 injured during the 2001 G8 summit in Genoa, Italy.

After the protests at the APEC conference in Vancouver, Chrétien's government did not take any chances. The G8 summit was held in Kananaskis, a secluded region of the Rocky Mountains. It was easy for the police to keep protesters out and the media coverage to a minimum in the remote area. The topics discussed at the meeting included the world economy, the international fight again terrorism, and the development of Africa.

During the Kananaskis summit, the "New Partnership for Africa's Development" and the "Africa Action Plan" were formed by the G8. Following the summit, Chrétien's government committed $6 billion to the development of Africa from 2002 to 2007. Canada's commitment to the Africa Action Plan resulted in the $500 million Canada Fund to Africa.

A large portion of the first G8 summit since the September 11 terrorist attacks was dedicated to discussing the challenges of fighting terrorism worldwide.

Relations with the United States

> "Canada and the United States have never agreed on every single issue of foreign policy. There have always been some trade disputes between us. No two countries, no two friends, agree on everything. Disagreement on a few issues between close friends is a sign of maturity, not a sign of a troubled relationship."
>
> *Chrétien, 2003*

I n his farewell speech in 2003, Chrétien claimed that pursuing an independent policy from the United States was one of the most positive elements of his term as prime minister. However, Canada's friendly relationship with the United States cooled considerably under his leadership.

The September 11, 2001, terrorist attacks on the United States impacted the world. The geographic **proximity** of the United States to Canada gave these attacks serious implications in terms of Canada's safety. Canada had become dependent on the U.S. market for its exports. After the 2001 attacks, crossing the U.S.-Canada border became an issue in regard to security measures.

Canada was expected to align with the United States' "war on terrorism." In March of 2003, the United States claimed that Iraq had weapons of mass destruction and invaded the Middle East country. When U.S. President George W. Bush did not obtain approval from the United Nations to invade Iraq, Chrétien refused to send Canadian troops. Most Canadians supported Chrétien's decision. Chrétien felt that the United States had not exhausted all possible alternatives.

The United States looked less favourably on the Canadian government, not only because of Chrétien's refusal to send troops, but also because of negative comments made about Bush by officials in Chrétien's government. The ambassador to Washington, Chrétien's nephew, said that it would have been better if Al Gore had won the 2000 Presidential election instead of George W. Bush.

Twenty-four Canadians died in the attacks on the World Trade Center buildings on September 11, 2001.

Chrétien's Legacy

> "So many memories. So many bonds and so many friendships. So much road travelled. For a young man born into a large working class family in Shawinigan. I am proud to say it is a road we have travelled together."
>
> *Chrétien's reflections on his time in government, November 13, 2003*

Chrétien served Canada as a politician for more than 40 years. He served with six prime ministers and held 12 ministerial positions. He won three consecutive Liberal majority governments. He was an experienced and savvy politician.

Chrétien's early years as prime minister were dominated by the Quebec referendum and a large federal debt left by the previous administration. By the time Chrétien retired from office, he had reduced the Canadian government's debt and put Canada on the forefront of international policies. Under Chrétien's leadership, Canada helped form the Arctic Council and hosted the APEC conference and G8 summit. In addition to Chrétien's commitment to environmental issues, such as preserving the Arctic environment, he worked to promote human rights at home and throughout the world.

His government established the University Millennium Scholarships, which provided funding for Canadians to obtain a post-secondary education.

Some politicians accused Chrétien of staying in power for so many years solely to ensure his place in Canadian history. In the end, however, his own members of Parliament deserted him, and his relations with his finance minister, Paul Martin, became strained. Without the support of his party, Chrétien was left with little choice but to resign.

In 1998, the Canadian Millennium Scholarship Foundation was created. The foundation has provided more than 1.6 billion in bursaries, awards, and scholarships to students.

Paul Martin:
The Effective Manager

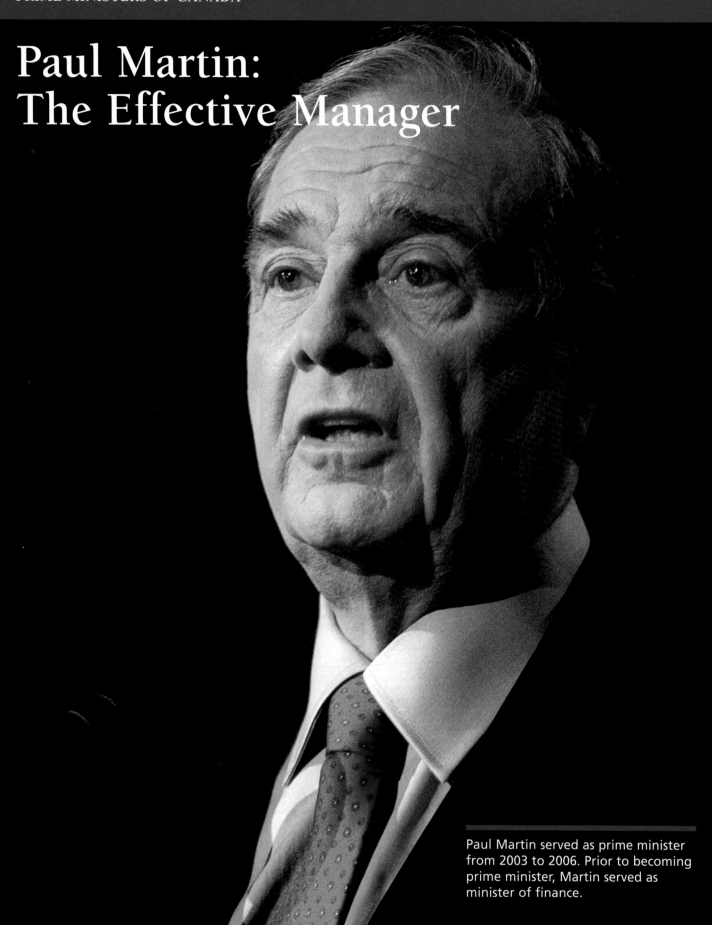

Paul Martin served as prime minister from 2003 to 2006. Prior to becoming prime minister, Martin served as minister of finance.

Paul Martin was born on August 28, 1938, in Windsor, Ontario, to Paul and Eleanor Martin. His father had served for 33 years in the House of Commons.

Martin entered the political arena and was first elected to Parliament in 1988. Two years later, he ran for the leadership of the Liberal Party but lost to Jean Chrétien. This was the beginning of a rivalry between Chrétien and Martin that lasted for more than a decade. Although they were rivals, Chrétien appointed Martin to be the minister of finance in 1993. Martin erased Canada's $42 billion debt, and, under his guidance, Canada had five consecutive surplus budgets.

On September 21, 2003, Martin was elected leader of the Liberal Party. He was immediately confronted with a report written by Auditor General Sheila Fraser. The report revealed that the Chrétien government had given contracts to individuals and firms in Quebec. The contracts had resulted in very little work. The Gomery Commission was launched to investigate the mismanagement of money by the Liberal government in what is now commonly referred to as the "Sponsorship Scandal." This scandal resulted in Martin gaining only a minority government after the June 2004 election.

In November 2005, the Gomery Commission cleared Paul Martin of any wrongdoing with respect to the Sponsorship Scandal, but the damage to the Liberal Party's reputation had already been done. A vote of non-confidence in November led to the election of January 23, 2006. For the first time in 18 years, the Conservative Party was elected. Martin had been prime minister for less than three years.

Although Martin's time in office was not long, he did achieve several positive measures. He passed the Civil Marriage Act, which made Canada the fourth country in the world to legalize same-sex marriages. Martin also established friendlier relations with the United States.

Before his political career, Martin was the president and owner of Canada Steamship Lines.

Keeping Canada Together

"We acted on the belief that Canada is strongest as a nation when we endeavor to ensure that no Canadian is ever left behind."
Paul Martin, concession speech, Montreal, January 23, 2006

Stephen Harper: Canada's 22nd Prime Minister

Stephen Harper was elected prime minister in 2006. He served as the leader of the Canadian Alliance from 2002 to 2004 and became leader of the Conservative Party of Canada in 2004.

Born on April 30, 1959, in Toronto, Ontario, Stephen Joseph Harper was one of three sons to Margaret and Joseph Harper. He attended high school at Central Etobicoke and graduated at the top his class in 1978.

Harper first became interested in politics in high school. He served as a member of his school's Young Liberal's Club. After high school, Harper moved to Calgary. He graduated from the University of Calgary with a Master of Arts degree in economics.

In 1985, Harper joined the PC Party as a legislative assistant on Parliament Hill. Frustrated with Brian Mulroney's government, Harper left the PC Party in 1986. The next year, Harper became a founding member of the Reform Party. When his relationship with Reform leader Preston Manning deteriorated, Harper resigned.

The Canadian Alliance Party was created in 2000 as successor to the Reform Party. In March 2002, Harper became the Party's leader. The following year, the PC and Canadian Alliance Parties joined to form the new Conservative Party of Canada. Harper led the Conservative Party in the 2004 federal election. The Conservatives lost to the Liberals. Less than two years later, Canadians again went to the polls. Paul Martin and the Liberal Party's campaign was affected by scandal. Harper campaigned on the reduction of GST and a childcare plan.

Harper became Canada's 22nd prime minister on February 6, 2006.

Harper grew up in Toronto, Ontario, home of the Blue Jays baseball team. He threw the first pitch at the June 22, 2004 game.

Keeping Canada Together

"Canada is uniquely blessed in the strength and diversity of its people and regions. Through hard work, foresight and good fortune, we have come together to make our vast country one of the most successful the world has ever seen."

Harper, Speech from the Throne, 2003

Timeline

1930s	1940s	1950s	1960s

PRIME MINISTERS

Brian Mulroney was born on March 20, 1939, in Baie-Comeau, Quebec. Chrétien was born on January 11, 1934, in Shawinigan Falls, Quebec.

Kim Campbell was born on March 10, 1947.

Brian Mulroney attended the Progressive Conservative leadership convention as a campus delegate from St. Francis Xavier in 1956.

Jean Chrétien was elected to the House of Commons in 1963.

CANADA

Cairine Wilson becomes the first woman senator, 1930.
The Canadian Broadcasting Company is created in 1936.
Canada declares war on Germany on September 10, 1939.

Canada declares war on Italy on June 10, 1940.
Canada joins the United Nations in 1945.

Canada sends troops to Korea in 1950.
The Massey Report into Canadian culture is released in 1951.

The maple leaf design becomes Canada's national flag in 1964. Canadians are issued social insurance cards for the first time on April 1964.

WORLD

Germany attacks Poland on September 1, 1939. Great Britain declares war on Germany on September 3, 1939,

Japan bombs Pearl Harbor on December 7, 1941.
D-Day takes place on June 6, 1944.

In 1957, the Soviet Union launches *Sputnik*, the first satellite successfully launched into space.

The Cuban Missile Crisis takes place in 1962. Martin Luther King Jr. is assassinated on April 4, 1968.

1970s | 1980s | 1990s

PRIME MINISTERS

Paul Martin becomes president of the Canada Steamship Lines in 1973.

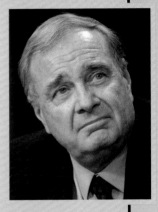

Brian Mulroney is elected prime minister of Canada on September 17, 1984.

Kim Campbell becomes Canada's first woman prime minister on June 25, 1993.

CANADA

The Toronto Blue Jays play their first game of baseball on April 7, 1976, against the Chicago White Sox.

Terry Fox, a cancer patient, runs in the Marathon of Hope in 1980 to raise awareness about cancer.

In 1999, Nunavut becomes Canada's third territory.

WORLD

Japanese soldier Shoichi Yokoi is discovered in Guam in 1972. He had been living in the jungle for 28 years.

The fall of the Berlin Wall occurs in November 1989.

Diana, Princess of Wales, is killed in the Pont de l'Alma road tunnel in Paris, France in 1997.

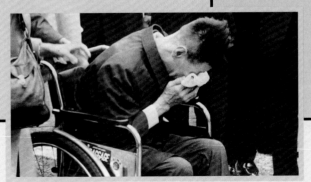

Did You Know?

In 2004, Kim Campbell was included in the list of the 50 most influential political leaders in the *Almanac of World History* compiled by the National Geographic Society.

All prime ministers, with the exception of Kim Campbell, have lived at 24 Sussex Drive during their terms of office.

In 1996, an aggressive protester approached Jean Chrétien, so the prime minister put him in a chokehold. This came to be known as the "Shawinigan handshake."

When U.S. President Ronald Reagan died in 2004, Brian Mulroney delivered the eulogy at his state funeral.

Stephen Harper is the first prime minister since Lester B. Pearson not to have attended law school.

Kim Campbell is only the second woman in history to sit at the table of the Group of Seven leaders (now G8), after British Prime Minister Margaret Thatcher.

Harper participated in the leaders debate at the National Arts Centre in Ottawa in 2004.

Test Your Knowledge

Question:
What prime minister influenced Brian Mulroney when he attended St. Francis Xavier University?

John Diefenbaker

Question:
Where is Jean Chrétien from?

Shawinigan, Quebec

Question:
Which two prime ministers from the contemporary period were born in Ontario?

Stephen Harper and Paul Martin

Multiple:
Kim Campbell was leader of what political party?

A) Liberal Party
B) Conservative Party
C) Parti Bloc Québécois

B) Conservative Party

Multiple:
What did Paul Martin legalize while in office?

A) same-sex marriage
B) the use of pepper spray
C) GST

A) same-sex marriage

Question:
What prime minister played a key role in forming the Conservative Party of Canada?

Stephen Harper

Question:
Which countries form the G8?

Britain, Canada, France, Germany, Italy, Japan, Russia, the United States

Question:
How many consecutive majority elections did Jean Chrétien win?

A) two
B) three
C) four

B) three

Question:
Who was known as Pierre Trudeau's "right-hand man"?

Jean Chrétien

Activity

MEECH LAKE ACCORD

The Meech Lake Accord specified the following:

- Quebec would be recognized as a distinct society within the Constitution.

- All provinces would have the right to recommend the appointment of Senators and **Supreme Court of Canada** justices.

- Changes to federal institutions, as well as changes from territories to provinces, would require approval by all Canadian provinces, as well as the Canadian Parliament.

- Provinces could opt out of newly created national social programs and receive federal revenues for their own social programs, as long as these met national objectives.

Which would you not support? Why?

CHARLOTTETOWN ACCORD

The Charlottetown Accord consisted of several points:

- It recognized Quebec as a distinct society with its own traditions.

- It recognized the idea of Aboriginal government on a par with federal and provincial governments.

- The Canadian **Senate** would be elected, not appointed.

- Canadian provinces would have extended powers, including power over social and health programs, as long as these were within "national standards."

Which would you not support? Why?

If Canada were to amend it Constitution, which accord should it adopt—the Meech Lake Accord or the Charlottetown Accord? Why?

Further Research

Books

To find out more about Canadian prime ministers, visit your local library. Most libraries have computers that connect to a database for researching information. If you input a key word, you will be provided with a list of books in the library that contain information on that topic. Non-fiction books are arranged numerically, using their call number. Fiction books are organized alphabetically by the author's last name.

Websites

The World Wide Web is also a good source of information. Reputable websites usually include government sites, educational sites, and online encyclopedias. Visit the following sites to learn more about Canadian prime ministers:

Study Canada's current prime minister and the political party in power on Government Canada's website.
www.pm.gc.ca

Check out short introductions, biographies, and quick facts on every prime minister from John A. Macdonald to Stephen Harper.
www.primeministers.ca

Look up prominent Canadian figures and politicians on the Dictionary of Canadian Biography Online.
www.biographi.ca/EN/index.html

Glossary

accord: an agreement

acid rain: toxic precipitation formed by air pollution

anglophones: English-speaking people, especially in a country where there is more than on official language

apartheid: in South Africa, the policy of economic and political separation of the native people from the rest of the population

bilingual: able to speak two languages

civil law: rules enforced by the government that protect the rights of citizens in a non-criminal capacity

civil service: people who work for the administration of the government

commission: a group of people appointed or elected with authority to do certain things

conservation: the official protection of the environment

francophone: French-speaking people, especially in a country where there is more than one official language

la Francophonie: a political organization of countries and people who use French in their domestic or international relations

moratorium: a legal authorization to delay payments of money

multicultural: the existence of several distinct cultural groups living within a country

Pacific Rim: the countries that border the Pacific Ocean

prosperity: good fortune or success

proximity: closeness

Quebeckers: people who live in or are from Quebec

reserve: land set apart for the exclusive use by Aboriginal Peoples

territory: a region or area of land

treaty: an agreement usually between two or more nations

Political Terms

cabinet minister: an elected member of Parliament chosen by the prime minister to be responsible for a specific area, for example, health or Aboriginal affairs

civil service: an organization of people who work for the administration of the government

Confederation: the event in 1867 when Canada became its own country.; the original four provinces were Quebec, Ontario, Nova Scotia, and New Brunswick

Conservative Party: a party that does not support radical change

criminal code: a group of government laws about justice, crime, and punishment

federal government: the government of the country, as opposed to provincial or municipal governments

federalists: people who agree with the national government's ideals and objectives

governor general: the representative of the British monarch in Canada

House of Commons: a government body made up of people who have been elected from across Canada to make laws for the entire country

Liberal Party: a party supporting moderate change and reform

Parliament: the House of Commons and the Senate

Parti Québécois: a separatist party

premier: a Canadian province's head of government

referendum: the process of submitting a law already passed by the lawmaking body to a direct vote of the citizens for approval or rejection

riding: an area or population represented by an elected member of parliament

Senate: a group of people made up of representatives from each province who review laws passed by the House of Commons

sovereignty: freedom from outside control

statesman: a person skilled in the management of public and national affairs

summit: a discussion or meeting between the heads of different governments

Supreme Court of Canada: the highest court in Canada

Index